# KALAMA

## Where Highway, Rail and Water Meet

Kopacetic inK

Copyright © 2006  City of Kalama  All rights reserved.

Printed in the United States of America by United Graphics Inc., Mattoon, Illinois

No part of this book may be used or reproduced in any manner whatsoever without written permission except in the case of brief quotations embodied in critical articles and reviews. For other permissions, fax (360) 425-1622.

Published and distributed by Kopacetic inK, Longview, Washington, USA

| | |
|---|---|
| Editor: | *Linda Beattie Inlow* |
| | *Louise Thomas* |
| Cover design: | *Another Jones Graphics* |
| Cover art: | *Screen Print Northwest* |
| Cover photographs: | *Cowlitz County Museum* |
| Inside photographs: | *Cowlitz County Museum* |
| | *Susy Campbell* |
| | *Linda Beattie Inlow* |
| Computer graphics & layout: | *Another Jones Graphics* |
| | *Kopacetic inK* |

The three cover photos and several of the older Kalama photographs in this book are used with permission of the Cowlitz County Museum.

First Printing ~ June 2006

City of Kalama
    Kalama, Washington : where highway, rail and water meet / Linda BeattieInlow, editor
        p. cm.
        Includes index
        ISBN 978-0-9619634-6-0
        1. History.  2. Washington History.  3. Tourism
        979.7

# KALAMA

## Where Highway, Rail and Water Meet

### Fun, Facts and Folklore

IN HONOR AND MEMORY OF THE
MEN AND WOMEN WHO FOUGHT
FIRES, SURVIVED FLOODS,
CAPITALIZED ON NATURAL
RESOURCES AND MAINTAINED
THE COMMUNITY KNOWN AS
**KALAMA**

## Acknowledgements

In 1990 the Kalama Centennial Celebration Committee had the foresight to publish a written history, <u>Kalama, Washington A Centennial History</u> edited by Violet Johnson. We are indebted to the persons who shared not only information for that publication with personal reflections, previously published articles and oral histories of our town, but also for the encouragement of inviting others to visit our community.

# Table of Contents

| | |
|---|---|
| A Community Welcome | 9 |
| A Brief History of Kalama | 15 |
| Totem Pole | 19 |
| Fact, Fiction or Folklore | 22 |
| Architectural History Tour | 31 |
| Glimpse of Kalama's Past | 53 |
| Information Guide | 67 |
|     Antique District | |
|     ATM | |
|     Automotive Services | |
|     Cemeteries | |
|     Government | |
|     Pharmacy | |
|     Recreation | |
|     Restaurants | |
|     Shopping | |
|     Service Organizations | |
| Calendar of Events | 81 |
| Kalama 2025 | 83 |
| Index | 85 |

# A Community Welcome

Following are on the street interviews from residents as well as those who work or own businesses in Kalama.

**What do you like about Kalama?**

Kalama has excellent schools, especially the elementary. Our family uses the Kalama River and the Marina Park. Kalama is a close knit community.

> Susie Janke
> Resident

Even though we are going through a growing spurt people have maintained their sense of community and that's very nice!

> Cindy Gleason
> Owner C. J.'s

Kalama is a proud little town, full of tradition and caring, community-minded families. Unlike many towns, it still has more churches than bars.

> Dawn Johnson-Deal, resident since 1965

There is so much I like about Kalama. The friendly people is one of the first things I think of. This is a real community. I graduated from Kalama High School, left for a brief time then came back. Now my grandchildren are in the Kalama School District. It amazes me how folks who don't even have kids come out to support our High School or community sports. This is a great place to live.

Linda Palmer<br>Kalama Shopping Center

Whether it is cheering for the High School football team, flanking the soccer fields or gathering at the loss of a loved one, Kalama's citizens have always supported my family.

Linda Durgeloh Williams<br>Life long resident

Our library has been a strong focal point in our community. People come to check their email, check out videos or audio books, and do research on the Internet. Several children are always present at our weekly reading programs sponsored by FOLK (Friends of the Library at Kalama) and many more participate in the summer reading adventure. Children and adults enjoy many fun activities sponsored by FOLK including author signings or book sales.

Theresa Barker<br>Resident and Treasurer of FOLK

Kalama Elementary is a small K-5 school of approximately 425 students from year to year. We have 3-4 classes at each grade level. We offer physical education, art, library, after school reading, and technology throughout the week in addition to regular education classes. The staff has created a compassionate professional learning community where each student is challenged to achieve and succeed at their level. It was selected as a recipient of the 2005 Apple Achievement Award by the State Board of Education for significant growth on the 2005 WASL. The 2004-05 fourth grade class, who earned the award for the school, averaged 24.9% growth over the previous year thrusting them into the top ten of 1142 elementary schools in the state. The student body chose to spend their $25,000.00 construction grant to add playground equipment to the play area.

This accomplishment was the most significant in my 36 year education career. It is something the community of Kalama should truly treasure as much as athletic accomplishments. It takes a village to raise a child, and we all have worked hard to provide for the children of the Kalama area.

Tom Eastwood
Principal Kalama Elementary

The first thing I noticed when we moved to Kalama were the friendly people.

Sue Seay *(pictured)*
Long time resident

Kalama is a great little town. I love its charm, but mostly the people. We live in one of the older houses in the downtown on a hill with a fabulous view of the river.

Carol Dunn
Kalama Resident

Hawaiians, like John Kalama, and his wife, Mary ,a Nisqually Indian have played a significant role in the development and cultural heritage of the Pacific Northwest. These contributions include: Fostering trade and commerce throughout the

Pacific Rim. As citizens of Kalama, we embrace our Hawaiian roots and can truly say, "Kalama - the little town with the big Aloha Spirit."

Don Purvis<br>City Councilman

Kalama is the San Francisco of Washington. It is a delightful community. My wife and I were attracted to the beautiful old Victorian and Craftsman style homes in the area, many of which over look the water.

We found an old Victorian house overlooking the river within walking distance of downtown and felt at home.

Dominic Ciancibelli<br>Custom Home Builder

There are some great examples of Victorian architecture with gables built at the turn of the century. Kalama is a small community, but serves up a great cup of coffee. The people are friendly. Growing up it seemed everybody knew everybody and people helped one another. Even though we are growing we still have that small town flavor.

Marc O'Neil<br>Manager J & B Towing

We moved here from Portland so my kids would be closer to their grandparents. Over the years we have become involved in sports. My boys were all in the wrestling program. I even coached baseball.

My family and I really enjoy the Community Fair. It's fun and the whole town turns out for the event.

Kalama has a real hometown atmosphere. Every Christmas the townspeople are invited to share Christmas dinner and Santa with the kids at a feast up at the school. Kalama has been a great town raise my boys.

Scott Merwin
Owner Kalama Hometown Hardware

One hour from Kalama and a person could be at the ocean, hiking or skiing in the mountains or travel to Portland or Longview for theater, shopping or traffic!

Coni McMaster
Kalama City Clerk

After retiring we moved to Kalama in 2004 for many reasons: close to an international airport, easy access to I-5, we wanted small town atmosphere, but a place that was growing and had many interests, yet was close to a big city. Portland is just 40 minutes away and Seattle 2.5 hours. Kalama is ideal.

Patti and Dan Ohall

I grew up here. People are always willing to help. Locals really support the businesses in the downtown area. That's nice.

BettyJean Bradford
Owner Just a Shot Away

*An early example of Kalama turn of the the century architecture*

# A Short History of Kalama

The original site of Kalama was wet, sandy and surrounded by rocks and trees. Kalama still boasts sandy beaches, lots of rocks, and a great variety of trees.

Kalama was strategically located at one of the deepest and narrowest points along the Columbia River. When the Federal Government established the donation Land Claim Law of 1850 several settlers took advantage and staked claims, 640 acres were given to married couples and 320 acres to single settlers.

Pioneer Ezra Meeker staked the first land claim. He built a small cabin next to a large rock outcropping where City Hall is now located. The large rock still looms behind. A replica of the Meeker cabin can be seen at the Kalama Fairgrounds west of town. Locals joke about the Kalama potatoes (rocks) that are still being tilled in vegetable and flower gardens.

Settlement of the Washington Territory boomed when the Northern Pacific Railroad selected Kalama as the western terminus of their railroad. The eastern terminus was at Duluth, Minnesota. Once the connection was complete in 1883 more pioneers journeyed to this area.

The City of Kalama prospered and the population grew to more than 4000 people by 1870. One steamboat brought 1300 Chinese to work on the railroad. They resided east of where the Kalama High School is now located. The road's name, China Garden, recalls this portion of Kalama's history.

Within a few months of the railroad expansion Kalama had car shops, machine shops, a round house, docks, stores, hotels, hospitals, sawmills, homes and seven saloons. Unlike the lawless

15

boomtowns of the West, the residents of Kalama must have had a strong religious background. The saloonkeepers were required to pay a portion of the ministers' salary! By 1870 the Methodists, Congregationalists and Catholics had churches in Kalama.

Kalama became the County seat for Cowlitz County in 1872, eventually relinquishing it to Kelso after sixteen years of heated debates in 1922. Old-timers suggest the seat was stolen in the dead of night, when the county offices at Kalama were raided and government papers were transported to Kelso.

The first economic disaster to hit Kalama was the 1872 movement of National Pacific Railroad's western terminus to Tacoma. The majority of the town's residents followed the railroad and moved north. Kalama's population dropped.

The second disaster occurred in 1879. A fire destroyed nearly ninety per cent of Kalama. Only a few homes remained along with the port buildings and the Catholic Church. In the following years three more devastating fires leveled various sections of the town. Floods plagued Kalama. One of the worst came in 1948 as the entire Columbia River flooded. In 1992 the lower section of town needed to be evacuated as water rose once again from under the city's streets. The north section of Main Street was again flooded including city offices, the library and police department.

When the railroad left Kalama turned to other industries like fishing, mining and logging. In 1892 just one company packed more than 1,400,000 pounds of sturgeon. Three years later, in 1895, Kalama was the site of the first State fish hatchery in the State of Washington. Built along the Kalama River the original hatchery has moved to Fallet Creek about three miles up the Kalama River. A larger hatchery is located another five miles beyond it. The hatcheries spawn Chinook, Coho and steelhead year round. They are open to the public. Call (360) 673-4825 for tour information.

Veins of ore including gold were discovered in the surrounding hills in the late 1800's. By the turn of the century many men came to work in mines. The mines soon closed as production costs exceeded profit.

Roads replaced rail and water for transportation by the early 1900's. In the 1880's the US Government surveyed roads used by soldiers. Like many historical communities Kalama has street names reflecting their history: Military Road, Cloverdale Road, China Garden, Meeker Drive, Modrow, and Green Mountain Road. The section of road between Kelso and Kalama was the last road paved to complete the link of highway stretching from southern Oregon to Canada.

Many well-known Americans have visited Kalama over the years including Theodore Roosevelt, Howard Taft, Jack Benny and Elvis Presley.

Today the center of Kalama is still nestled along the hillside next to the Columbia River, railroad and Interstate 5. The steeple from St. Joseph's Catholic Church is a landmark. The residential community has spread along to the north along the Kalama River, to hillsides behind and above the Kalama High School and to the south along Cloverdale Road and up Green Mountain Road. Since 2000 several new neighborhoods have been developed as farm or timberland have been converted to residential housing

Today the city of Kalama boasts an extensive antique district, several good restaurants and eateries, a hardware store, a bank, a credit union, lawyer and dentist offices, a grocery store, a video store, a real estate office, four churches, several parks, a marina, campsites, recreational opportunities, an elementary, middle school and high school.

*View of Columbia River, I-5 and Railway*

As it was in its early years Kalama is still a town where
HIGHWAY, RAIL AND WATER MEET.

## TOTEM POLE
### located at Kalama Marina Park

Chief Lelooska, a.k.a. Don Smith, of Ariel, Washington began carving the tallest of these three totem poles in 1961. It is the tallest totem pole made from a single tree. He carved all three totem poles for Kalama.

19

Many commuters driving along Interstate 5 in the early sixties saw him carving the 140-foot, 20,000-pound cedar log.

The totem pole carvings serve as lineage crests and illustrate legends. The tallest pole is a close replica to the Sakau'wan chief of the Gitrhawn clan at the former village of Gwunwawq in British Columbia.

An eagle tops the totem pole. Under him is Man-Underneath, a supernatural being seen by ancestors of the clan in their southward migrations on the Alaskan coast. Next is Shark, then Unwait, another supernatural figure that was changed to Beaver on this pole. Next is the Dragon-Fly with a long sharp nose followed by Bullhead, a monster of the sea with a human face depicted on its tail.

The next two figures represent ancestors, Aitl and Gunas, who drowned at sea. The twelfth figure is a Devil Fish with a second Man-Underneath who is above the Grizzly Bear.

The bottom figure is Flying-Frog. Small faces adorn its ribs and body while the Man holds the Frog's hind legs.

The totem poles can be viewed at Kalama Marine Park. More information is available under the covered picnic area near the totem poles.

*Directions: From the north – Exit 30 KALAMA, turn right, then right again winding around underneath the off ramp. Continue south about one mile, turning left just past the marina. A parking lot for the Marina Park will be straight ahead or off to the right.*
*From the south – Exit 27 TODD RD/PORT OF KALAMA, turn left go under the overpass, turn right, turn right again just past the railroad tracks continue for about 2 miles, just past the RV sites is the Marina Park. Parking will be available next to picnic area, baseball field or playground.*

*Marina Park near the Totem Poles is an ideal place for kids to play, have a picnic under shelter, play some softball, walk the beach or just sit and enjoy the river.*

# FACT, FICTION or FOLKLORE?

1. Logging was never a major industry in Kalama.

2. Kalama became a boomtown overnight.

3. Kalama was named after John Kalama.

4. Ezra Meeker, not John Kalama, staked the first claim on the present site January 20, 1853.

5. The railroad played an important part in building Kalama.

6. *Minnetonka* was the name of the ferry connecting the railroad in Goble, Oregon to the railroad in Kalama.

7. The first settlers helped to build the railroad along the Cowlitz Corridor.

8. The first edition of a published paper was the "Cowlitz Bulletin."

9. Kalama was so heavily populated at one time with people from the Midwest a part of the town was nicknamed "Nebraska Hill."

10. Robert Day was hung at 11:15 AM on June 3, 1892 behind the courthouse in Kalama.

11. In 1915 Kalama Telephone was owned by Kalama Electric Light and Power and was managed by George Coffey. It had 196 telephones.

12. Gold was discovered and mined in Kalama.

*This view from S. 2nd shows the Columbia River, the marina (covered area near river), and a part of Main Street. The far right in the middle is a small portion of the industrial park. Across the river is the State of Oregon.*

# ANSWERS to FACT, FICTION or FOLKLORE

1. FICTION - Logging was the first industry for the fledgling town of Kalama. Prior to the first settlement steamers were engaged in the transportation of freight and passengers along the Columbia River from Vancouver to Cowlitz Landing on the Cowlitz River. The vessels needed cord wood to burn as fuel.

The settlers in Kalama and south towards Martin's Bluff cut cord wood and hauled it with the help of white and Oriental labor to the one wood dock at Kalama and three others on the river bank south of that point. The cord wood industry was the principal source of revenue for early settlers.

Although no longer a primary source of income loaded logging trucks still traverse Kalama River Road, Cloverdale, Old Pacific Highway and Green Mountain Roads bringing their timber to mills in the surrounding area.

2. FACT - In 1870 the Northern Pacific Railway unloaded a mountain of supplies and 1300 laborers at the Kalama dock. Kalama became the western terminus for the railroad. Suddenly streets and lots covered the flat land and climbed the hill. According to a brochure printed by North Pacific Grain Growers a sign along the river proclaimed KALAMA - WHERE RAIL MEETS SAIL.

3. Technically FOLKLORE - General Sprague named the town "Kalama" in 1871 after the river two miles to the north. *The Kalama River was named Kalama after John Kalama,* a full-blooded Hawaiian, who was born in Kula, Maui around 1814. He was hired by the Hudson Bay Company and arrived in the Pacific Northwest ca.1830 aboard a fur-trading vessel. He married

Mary, the daughter of a Nisqually Indian Chief. They settled in an area near the mouth of what is now known as the Kalama River. Noted for his carpentry, farming and trapping skills, John worked at Fort Vancouver and was housed for a time at the Kanaka village next to the fort, before being assigned to other locations as operations gradually shifted to the North. He also worked on the Cowlitz Farm and at Fort Nisqually.

In 2005, the City of Kalama held a celebratory event – *The Kalama Days of Discovery*, marking the 175th anniversary of the coming of John Kalama to the Pacific Northwest. The 4 living grandchildren of John and Mary Kalama were honored at this Hawaiian and Native American-themed event. The Days of Discovey will be an annual event held in August, which is open to the public.

4. FACT - Ezra Meeker built a log cabin on the big rock on the East side of First Street. The stake was located on what was once the back of the Carlson Opera House and Harned's Drug Store (now the back of the Kalama Telephone Company building). Meeker lived there for a year. None of the original buildings remain. A replica, however, is on loan at the Kalama Fairgrounds located just off Interstate 5 at Exit 32.

Ezra Meeker and his family traveled from Ohio to Oregon in 1851. He arrived in Portland with $2.75 in his pocket. The Meeker family moved to St. Helens to help Ezra's brother, Oliver with his boarding house. In January 1853 with business tapering off the brothers rowed to the other side of the river where on January 20, 1853 Ezra staked his claim.

Ezra eventually settled in Puyallup, Washington where his home is a museum. The road leading west out of Kalama towards the Kelso community of Carrolls bears his name.

5. FACT. The railroad played an important part in building Kalama.

The first spike of the Pacific Division of the Northern Pacific Railroad was driven in Kalama on May 19, 1871. Thousands of workers and dollars came to Kalama to build 25 miles of railroad. The railroad was completed in 1873. Workers were paid $2.25 a day, a good wage of the time.

6. FALSE. The *Tacoma* was the name of the ferry connecting Goble rail located in Oregon to the Northern Pacific Railroad in Kalama. This iron ferry was shipped around Cape Horn the southernmost tip of South America and assembled in a Portland shipyard in 1884. The Tacoma, a 334-foot side-wheeler, was purported to be the second largest ferry in the world at that time. A pilothouse was at either end.

The *Tacoma* was a rail transfer ferry. She was 76 feet wide and had a capacity of 27 freight cars or 15 passenger cars. She ferried trains until 1908 across the Columbia River where they continued their journey north to Puget Sound.

The trains traveled each way once a day boasting a combination of freight and passenger cars.

The *Minnetonka No. 84* was the first locomotive brought to Kalama for use in building the road. Upon completion of the road in 1895 the *Minnetonka* was sold to Polson Logging Company in Hoquiam, Washington where she became known as "Old Betsy." Temporarily forgotten and abandoned the Northern Pacific located the No. 84 in the woods near Hoquiam. The Minnetonka was restored and displayed at the World Fairs in New York and Chicago in the 1930's. Today her permanent home is in St. Paul, Minnesota.

7. FACT and FICTION. The first settlers helped to build the railroad along the Cowlitz Corridor, but the majority of workers (about 1000) were Chinese. China Garden Road (above Elm Street and past the High School) commemorates these hard workers as well as identifies where many of the Chinese laborers lived.

8. FACT. The first edition of a published paper was the "Cowlitz Bulletin". At one time five papers were being published, but only the Kalama Bulletin survived. It was predominantly owned and operated by early pioneer Hite Imus until 1917.

9. FICTION. Kalama was populated at one time with people from the Midwest. The northeast corner was nicknamed *"Kansas Hill."* The photo below is of "Kansas Hill" today.

Many of these Kansas settlers came to Kalama by personal invitation. Current residents described the increase of port development, the expansion of the fishing industry, and a fish canning plant to friends and family in Kansas and other midwestern states. Their promotion of recreational activities and the possibility of mining encouraged several families to journey west.

10. FACT. Robert Day was hung at 11:15 AM on June 3, 1892 behind the courthouse in Kalama. Over 300 people crowded into town to witness the event. Not only was this the first public hanging to take place in Cowlitz County, it was the first legal execution in the State of Washington.

Robert Day was hung for the murder of Thomas Clinton Beebe on October 9, 1891. The newspaper of that day stated Day "mounted the steps leading to the scaffold with a firm step, unfettered and unassisted and standing by the rope and noose began a 20 minute talk by saying 'How do you do gentleman, my business here is to be hung.'"

11. FACT. In 1915 the Kalama Telephone, owned by Kalama Electric light and Power and managed by George Coffey, had 196 telephones. Today Kalama Telephone is still family owned and headquartered in Tenino, Washington and offers Internet service, DSL, web hosting and has 3000+ telephones in the Kalama area.

12. FACT. Gold was discovered at what is now the end of Fir Street. The Darnell Mine and other mining ventures petered out due to the inaccessibility of the ore. The cost of production exceeded any profit.

*Kalama High School's stadium and track field is close to site of the Darnell Mine.*

*This is the old Cloverdale Schoolhouse. It served the outlying community as a one room school with classes first through sixth grades for several years until the students were bused into Kalama. The building was bought by the Kalama Lion's Club and moved in the early 1990's to its present Cloverdale location. The building is leased by Helping Hands, a community service organization.*

Even new construction as the Olson building above holds a flavor of Kalama's past as does the architecture of the local post office below.

# Architectural History Tour

### 454 Second

Designed as a private residence and currently in use as such, this house, which has been altered, is in good condition. The structure, built about 1892, is a visually striking residence in Kalama. Its position overlooking town and highway renders it one of the most important parts of Kalama's architectural identity. The design of this house, particularly the turret, has no equivalent in Cowlitz County. The design of the house was unique at the time it was built, as it had the first turret in Kalama. It sits on a bedrock hillside. Second Avenue, rising up the hill, fronts the residence. Its most distinctive feature is a multisided conical roof over a polygonal bay porch, reached by climbing ten wooden stairs, which extend along the house front, around the turret, and along the east side of the house to the kitchen. When this house was built, the porch extended clear to the back corner of the house and enclosed a natural well, which provided water for the house. At some point, the porch was framed in to enlarge the kitchen, and the well was covered. Turned columns support the porch roof with decorative trim above. The house plan is a rectangle oriented west to east. A small extension is just west of the front door. Its roof is a gable with a returned roofline. The gable end is decorated with shingling in a fishscale pattern - a pattern, which also appears below the roofline in other parts of the house.

## Northern Pacific Railroad Hospital
### 415 N. Third

Built in 1872, the old Northern Pacific Railroad Hospital building is the sole remaining structure from that era. Altered and in good condition it is now used as a private residence. This two-story basically rectangular building is highlighted by its bellcast mansard roofline. The main entrance facing North Third features two doorways. There is a covered porch supported by squared posts which runs the length of the front of the house. A decorative railing on the top of the porch is flat and runs to the base of the bellcast mansard roof. The rear of the house features two polygonal bays with a door and closed deck between. The door features stained glass windows with a flush blind transom.

### 308 Second Street

This home was designed and built in 1900 and remains a private residence today. The building is unaltered and in good condition. Two and one half stories, the house has a basically square plan. High on the hillside above Kalama's commercial district, it joins the "Turret House" as unique examples of 19$^{th}$ century architecture. Its complex gable roofline faces 2nd Avenue. Shingles decorate the roof's gable ends. The main floor turns into a three-sided bay to the west of the front door.

The second floor overhang is decorated with wood trim. Wooden railings line the wooden front steps and the covered porch. Turned columns support the porch roof. Turned trim lines and the porch roof line contrast

with the shiplap siding. The front door has window and is surmounted by a simple transom.

The Imus family, a noted local family, owned this home for over 40 years. The Imus family was intrinsic in developing Kalama from 1889 onward.

## Storie Mansion
### 650 Fir Street

Unaltered and in excellent condition, this original residence is currently being used as a private residence. The Sisters of Charity of the House of Providence purchased the land originally from the Lake Superior

and Puget Sound Co. In 1909, the Wilson-Case Lumber Co. purchased the land and Willard Case had an 18-room mansion designed and built. Many materials for the mansion were imported and specially made. The building has multiple decorative features. It is a rectangular three-story home with a bellcast hipped roof with multiple dormers on all sides. The house features a covered entrance with a balcony above it.

The mansion home is nestled among fir trees high on the hill overlooking the Kalama High School, downtown Kalama and the Columbia River.

## St. Joseph's Catholic Church
### Fourth Street Near Elm Street

Unaltered and in good condition St. Joseph's is still in use as a church. There has been a Catholic Church building on the same site since the 1870's. The Franciscan Order of Priests of the Catholic Church constructed the present building in 1909. It sits with its simple beauty high on a hill overlooking the city of Kalama and the Columbia River.

A city landmark, the church is wood frame with gabled roof and shiplap siding. Rectangular in design, it has five Gothic style windows along each main side of the building with a single centered spire on the facade of the church. The side windows feature a two-center transom for opening. The church has appeared on the State Register since 1979.

Mass is held on Saturday evening.

### 356 Elm

This site was purchased by the School District No. 10 in 1875 from the Lake Superior & Puget Sound Company. A schoolhouse was built in 1890. The building now a private residence remains unaltered and in good condition. It is a rectangular structure with a gabled roof and shiplap siding. The windows are of the double-hung, two sashes, and two-paned. The main entrance faces Elm Street. There is a covered porch supported by wood posts, which runs the length of the house and around the west side.

## Former Masonic Lodge
## 160 Third

The Masonic Lodge was erected in 1922 and used as a lodge hall until 1995. It remains unaltered and in excellent condition. This is a rectangular two-story structure. Its gabled end is on the front and faces west on Third Street. The first floor is brick and the second floor is covered with natural wood shakes. A gabled roof covers the porch with two posts as support. There is the same natural shake on the porch gable as on the main house. The Kalama Masons were one of the first chartered lodges in the State of Washington. Getting its charter in 1871, most of the masons in Cowlitz County were under their jurisdiction until the 1920's when charters were approved in many other towns. The present lodge, built in 1922, used some materials from the original lodge.

The building was sold in 1995. It is currently a private residence. The Masonic emblem formerly on the home was replaced with a decorative wood sculpture.

## 145 Fir Street

This building was constructed in 1890 by John Seibert, a Kalama Councilman. Built for commercial use it is not known what type of store or shop occupied the main floor. The second floor housed living quarters or apartments. An outside stairway on the west side leads to the second floor.

The shop was built partway up a hill for protection from floodwaters. Locally significant as an historical structure, this is a two-story rectangular structure with the gabled end facing the street. The gabled end has decorative shingles under it. This house is sided with shiplap. The covered front entrance has fixed single pane windows.

In the recent past this home served both as a residence and business.

### 180 SECOND STREET

This private residence was built in 1890 and has remained unaltered and in good condition. This home certainly typifies the building styles of its era. It is a two-story, wood frame house with the gabled roof facing west on Second. The siding is shiplap with fishscale decorative shingles in the gabled end from midway up the second floor windows. There is a polygonal bay on the northwest side of the house.

## COMMUNITY BUILDING
### CORNER OF 2ND AND ELM ST.

In 1870, the railroad built a 3-story hotel called the Kazano House. Three years later, Kalama became the county seat and the Kazano House became the county courthouse.

In 1922, Kelso succeed in taking the county seat from Kalama. The old courthouse was torn down. Materials salvaged from the demolition, wood windows, etc. were used to build the present Community Building in 1934. The construction was part of a W.P.A. project.

The Community Building has a large ballroom with stage, a smaller clubroom, a complete kitchen, two bathrooms and storage rooms on the main floor. There is a basement and more rooms on the second floor.
In the past portions of the building were used for Head Start programs and during one recent flood the ballroom became the library.

The building is presently used for community functions and rented for private events.

## 172 Second Street

This picturesque home was built in 1890 as a private residence.

The home was built after Washington statehood and the incorporation of Kalama as a fourth class town. It is still a private residence. It has been remodeled several times, but retains its original architectural style.

CORNER OF FIRST STREET AND FIR

This building was erected in 1896 as a commercial building. It presently houses businesses. It is rectangular with a classic western false front made of shiplap siding. Display windows extend along the entire front of the building.

There is a two foot brick foundation along the front. The building's concrete steps go up to the recessed entrance's glass door. The side panels along the entry way are made of glass.

Worn wood floors, a wooden rail which runs around the upper interior floor from the stairs and long wooden counters reflect the commercial history of this building. The building is a keystone of Kalama's Antique District. The vacant lot (where the car is parked) once hosted an apartment/hotel building.

### H. W. KOCKRITZ BUILDING

This three-story brick structure stands next to Heritage Square. The H. W. Kockritz building was constructed in 1908 as a restaurant and hotel. It has been remodeled repeatedly over the years. The front of the building has a boxed cornice decorative frieze with brackets at the end. The building presently houses businesses on the first floor and apartments above.

*W.H. Kockritz as it stands today is still used as an eatery on the first floor with apartments above.*

## 260 Elm Street

George Duvall, a Civil War Veteran, built this home at 260 Elm in 1890. Its original colors were red, white, and blue. This house represents the architecture of its era. The second story balcony was not part of the original design.

Captain George Gore, skipper of the ferry "Tacoma" which transported trains from Kalama, Washington to Goble, Oregon, later purchased the house from Duvall

## 160 First Street

This private residence was built in 1900. It is a two story, "L"-shaped residence with a gabled roof following the same design. There is a gabled dormer in the center of the front, which is supported by two posts and forms a covered balcony with two windows and a door. The entrance faces west.

On the north side of the building under the gable there is an inset balcony with a door and two windows.

Decorative shingles cover the gabled ends and the dormer. The exterior siding is shiplap.

The unique architecture can be attributed to the builder, John Larson. Mr. Larson was a mate on the "Tacoma", the ferry used by the Northern Pacific Railroad to transport complete trains across the Columbia River. The second floor balconies reflect his interest in the Columbia River.

### 196 First Street

Mr. Dunn, a carpenter for the railroad, built this home around 1897. He and his wife raised two daughters and a son in Kalama. Between 1903 and 1906 the original kitchen, dining area and one upstairs bedroom was enlarged to include a first story front room with two tiny bedrooms directly above it.

The home remained in the Dunn family until Raymond Dunn's death in the 1970's. It has since passed through several owners.

In 1979 extensive renovation took place. The interior was gutted restored.

The first floor dining room houses a wood stove in the same location as the original kitchen's wood stove. Oak and mahogany are prevalent throughout the interior. The ceiling heights vary throughout the home indicating repeated remodeling.

Although much of the first floor is hidden behind the hedges, the home still commands a beautiful view of the Columbia River and Kalama Marina.

## SECOND AVENUE SOUTH

The homes on Second Avenue South can be seen from the river, highway and rail. The following photos are prime examples of the Victorian architecture as well as some Craftsman style homes which were popular at the turn of the century when Kalama became a thriving community.

*These homes were built at the turn of the century. Many of the interiors have been updated and a few restored.*

*The home above was built in 1910. The home below sits away from the street. It began as the Methodist Church's parsonage and is now a private residence.*

Some remodeling has been done to update these homes, but for the most part they remain true to the original builder's plan. Each commands a view of the river, is within walking distance to downtown, the schools, shopping and has easy access to the highway.

# Glimpses of Kalama's Past

The building once used to hang the fire hose was located near the top of Elm Street. It no longer exists. The fire department is now located on Frontage Road in the heart of downtown Kalama. Fire Department substations are in outlying areas.

We wish to thank the Cowlitz County Museum located in Kelso, Washington and Mrs. Susy Campbell for sharing these pictures of Kalama's past.

In the above photograph the fire hose building can be seen at the center right. The streets are still dirt, but houses dot the hillside. Lots were orinally measured in 25 feet widths.

The lower left photo is of downtown Kalama. Many of these buildings are still standing. The town was built on stilts to accomodate the Columbia River tide. As time progressed the tide lands were filled. It is rumored even locomotives from the railway era are buried beneath 1st Street. The above photo shows the tide lands; the one below what Kalama looked like when the tidelands were filled.

The above photo is another look at 1st Street. The Kockritz building and Cloninger (now Heritage Square) are on the right.

Below is an interior photo of the restaurant inside the Kockritz building in the 1900's.

The ferry *Tacoma* played an important part in Kalama's history. She brought complete trains from Goble, Oregon to off load at Kalama where the trains continued northward.

The photo below is of the railroad tracks inside the *Tacoma*.

57

Above: An aerial view of one of the four floods which plagued Kalama. The cluster of buildings in the center are on Fir and 1st Street.

Below: During the 1948 flood. The operator for George Coffey's telephone company had to be rowed to work!

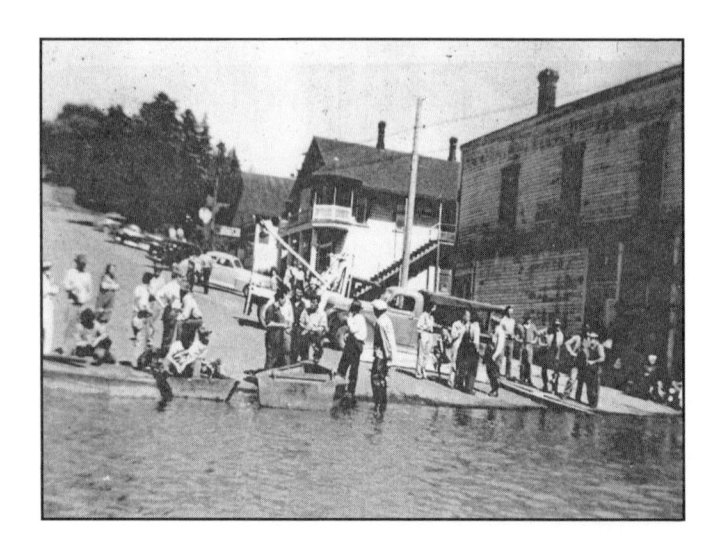

Fire threatened to destroy portions of Kalama more than once. Each time she rose up and built again.

Above is a photo of the first hydro electric plant in Kalama. Note the fisherman in the lower left corner! Many things have brought people to Kalama over the years: fishing, recreation, politics, building the railroad or a booming community. Theodore Roosevelt (below) made a whistle stop at Kalama on his campaign trail and Elvis Presley spent the night at what is now the Kalama River Inn on his way to Seattle.

# CHURCHES

## St. Joseph's Catholic Church

Mass
5:00 PM
Saturday

St. Joseph's Catholic Church was one of the six mission churches belonging to the Cowlitz Prairie Missions. Mass has been offered at St. Joseph's since 1874, although records have been located indicating Father Blanchett, a missionary, was in this area in 1838. The 1876 the Church was built on wood cribbing, but by 1909 deterioration necessitated the building of a new church on the old site. The current building was completed in 1909. Further repairs to the foundation were made in 2005.

The location of the structure at the top of 4th and Elm St. spared it from the numerous fires which plagued Kalama. The hilltop location made the Catholic Church a navigational landmark to the *Tacoma* ferry as she came across the Columbia River from Goble, Oregon. St. Joseph's is still easily recognized from river, rail and highway.

The building is an example of Stick Style architecture.

## Kalama United Methodist Church
111 N. 2nd St.
Worship 11:00 AM Sundays

The Methodist Church was organized in 1871 with a membership of nine and a pastor's salary of $60. The church has had several locations. Fire destroyed the various church buildings four times. The second church was built with donated lumber on unstable ground and gave way in a storm.

By 1890 with no current church building the Kalama United Methodist Church had only an occasional service (about once a month) and no Sunday school. The congregation met in the schoolhouse.

The small congregation, which offered a salary of $146.00 per month to the pastor, started the third building in 1894. Unfortunately it burned in 1895 just prior to completion with a thousand dollar indebtedness and no insurance.

The members met for prayer meetings in the courthouse where the Community Building now stands. In 1897 under new pastoral leadership the members worked to pay off the debt and build the fourth church. The new pastor earned $273.00 per month.

During construction services were again held in the schoolhouse. Membership grew to more than 80 people by the time the new building was completed in 1901. In 1928 a spark from a bonfire burned the fourth church building.

The current Methodist Church was erected in 1929. It was also the parsonage for the pastor and family. The parsonage area is currently used as a pre-school and Sunday school rooms.

## Church of the Nazarene
501 Cloverdale Rd
Sunday School 9:45 AM
Worship 10:45 AM and 6:00 PM
360 673 3581

Three families attended the first meeting to organize a church. They met in a saloon on First St. where ten-year-old Myrtle Westerlund played the pump organ. They later moved to the Congregational Church at the base of the hill on 2$^{nd}$ St. In 1918 Rev. Frank Blackman, a pastor in Ridgefield held services on Sunday afternoons. The Nazarene Church was officially organized with 12 charter members.

Land became available in 1920 across from the Methodist Church. Chester Orem donated standing timber for the church. Lumber was hewn and nailed by volunteers to build what is now Rivertown Antiques.

At one time the building housed the parsonage in the basement. The above photo shows the Church at its present Cloverdale location. The Church of the Nazarene historically and presently hosts a strong music, youth and education program.

In the late 1960's Pastor Salisbury helped the church purchase the land where the current Church is located. Pastor Adams was called and oversaw the construction at its current location. The congregation moved from downtown to Cloverdale in 1972.

## Kalama Baptist Church
Southern Baptist Congregation
112 Vincent Rd
Sunday School 9:45 AM
Worship Service 11:00 AM and 7:00 PM
360 673 5570

Following an initial telephone survey asking for interest in starting a Baptist church in April of 1979, the people met at the old Grange Hall (shown below) on Vincent Road. On June 25, 1979 their first Vacation Bible School began. Associational Missionary David C. Bandy led the mission congregation.

Five persons, Richard and Carmen Alford, Sherry and Jerry Lozier and Mike Newman, constituted the charter membership of Kalama Baptist Church.

Pastor Walter Grubbs served as the Baptist minister from July 1979 until June of 1980 when Pastor Tim Gillihan took over.

In 1980 the Grange Hall building became officially Kalama Baptist Church. Mel Suddeth was pastor in 1984 when the missionary congregation petitioned for independence. The membership had grown from 5 to 50.

Pastor Wes Eader came to the pulpit in December 1987 and as of 2006 still pastors the church.

## ANTIQUES – DEALERS

### Columbia Antiques & Collectibles
364 N 1st St.
Kalama 360 673 5400

### Drew & Davis Antiques
222 N 1st St.
Kalama 360 673 4029

### Forget Me Not Antiques
413 N 1st St.
Kalama 360 673 1525

### Heritage Square
176 N 1st St.
Kalama 360 673 3980

### Judy's Antiques
154 N 1st St.
Kalama 360 673 4415

### Memory Lane Antique Mall
199 N 1st St.
Kalama 360 673 3663

### The Country Gentleman
413 N 1st St.
Kalama 360 673 6720

### The Mouse House Antiques & Collectibles
297 N 1st St. #C
Kalama 360 673 6130

67

### Old Friends Antiques
297 N 1st St.
Kalama          360 673 3223

### Rivertown Antique Market
155 Elm St.
Kalama          360 673 2263

### Thelma's This N That
413 N 1st St.
Kalama          360 673 3474

## ATM

### Kalama Chevron Station
344 NE Frontage Road
Kalama, WA     360 673 2972

**Cowlitz Bank**
195 N 1st St.
Kalama   360 673 2226

**Fibre Federal Credit Union**
384 N 1st St.
Kalama   360 423 8750

## AUTO SERVICES

**Kalama Auto Supply**
344 NE Frontage Rd
Kalama, WA   360 431 0609
Food, Fuel

## CEMETERIES

**Kalama Cemetery** (IOOF)
Cemetery Road
*Directions: Off Exit 32, right on Elm,*
*Left on 2nd which becomes Spencer Creek*
*about 2.8 miles Cemetery Rd is on left hand side.*

**Martin's Bluff Cemetery**
Martins Bluff Rd
*Directions: Exit 27, Turn right on Todd Rd about 1 mile turn*
*right on Cloverdale Rd. Drive about 1.3 miles and Martin*
*Bluff is on the right.*

# GOVERNMENT

## Cowlitz County Fire District 5
382 NE Frontage Road
Kalama    360 673 2222
Ccfd5@kalama.com

## Kalama City Hall
City Council Chambers
Council meets every other Wednesday 7 pm
320 N. 1st
Kalama    360 673 3265
www.cityof kalama.com

**Kalama High School**
Home to the Chinooks
www.kalama.k-12.wa.us

## Kalama School District
Elementary, Middle School and High School
548 China Garden Rd
Kalama    360 673 5225

## Kalama Public Library
*FREE Internet Access*
*Hours: Noon to 5:00 pm*
*Monday through Saturday*
312 N 1st
Kalama    360 673 4568

## US Postal Service
454 N. 1st St
Kalama    360 673 3567

## LODGING
### Best Value Kalama River Inn
*Exit 30 on Frontage Rd*
602 NE Frontage Rd
Kalama    360 673 2855

## RECREATION

### Kress Lake
*Fishing, non-motorized Boating, Walking Paths*
Old US 99
Fish & Wildlife Parking Permit required
*Directions: Exit 32 – Right, next left past fairgrounds*

## Kalama Community Fairgrounds
Soccer/Baseball Fields
*Kalama Fair 2nd weekend in July*
Old US 99
PO Box 546
Kalama          360 673 5323
*Directions: Exit 32 – Right, then left on Old Pacific Hwy*

## Camp Kalama RV Park
Overnight/Long Term Stays, Store, Restaurant
5055 Meeker Drive
*Directions: Exit 32 – Right, then take next right for about ¼ mile, Camp Kalama will be on left*

## Washington State Fish Hatcheries
Upper and Lower Kalama River
Coho, Chinook and Steelhead.
OPEN TO PUBLIC.
Tours available.
(360) 673-4825

## Washington Fish & Wildlife Boat Launch
Primitive Boat Launch
W. Kalama River Road - Exit 32
Fish & Wildlife Parking Permit required

## Dick Maruhn City Park
Covered Picnic Area
Frontage Road
*Directions: Exit 30 – Park is at north end of town.*

**Toteff Park** (pictured above)
Covered Picnic Area, Playground
Elm Street/1$^{st}$ Street
*Directions: Exit 30 – Park is at south end of town.*

**Port of Kalama Marina**
Public Boat Launch, Marine Fuel, Long/Short Term Moorage, Showers, Boardwalk 
*Directions:*
***From north***
*– Exit 30 –*
*Turn right,*

take next right and keep right, paralleling the freeway
**From south** – Exit 27 – Turn left, go under the overpass, turn right paralleling the freeway and train tracks, Marina will be @ 3 miles north on left across from center of town.

## Port of Kalama Marine Park
*Home of tallest totem pole in the world!*
140-foot single tree totem pole carved by the late Chief Don Lelooska of Ariel, Washington.
Totem Poles, Restrooms, Picnic Shelters, Lewis & Clark Monument, Baseball Field, Walking Paths, Playground

## Kalama Community Building
Kitchen, Ballroom, Stage
Rental available for events
360 673 4564
*Directions: Exit 30 –* **From north** *– Continue straight paralleling freeway, at stop turn left, two blocks up on left.*

*From south* – *Turn right at stop sign, two blocks up on left.*

## PHARMACY

### Godfrey's Pharmacy
270 N 1st
Kalama, WA    360 673 2600

## RESTAURANT/FOOD SERVICE
*Following are listed from the North to South end of Town*

### from EXIT 32

### Fireside Café                               B/L/D
5055 Meeker Dr.
Kalama            360 673 2456
campkalama@kalama.com

Directions: Exit 32 – East of freeway at Camp Kalama

## from EXIT 30
### The Port Espresso
1230 N Hendrickson Drive
Kalama 360 673 3399
*Exit 30 – from north turn right, next right and shop is by the service station*
*From south –take left at stop sign under the overpass, turn right, at stop sign turn left, then next right towards service station*

### Columbia Inn Restaurant    B/L/D
698 NE Frontage Rd
Kalama 360 673 7600
*Exit 30 – North end of town, east of freeway*

### CJ's on the North Side    Lunch
550 N 1st
Kalama 360 673 2401
*Espresso * Deli * Laundromat*

### Kalama Burger Bar    L/D
49 Ivy St.
Kalama 360 673 2091

### Antique Deli    Lunch
413 N 1st St.
Kalama 360 673 3310

### Kalama Chevron
Food Mart – Deli - Espresso
344 NE Frontage Rd
Kalama 360 673 2972

RESTAURANT/FOOD SERVICE

## RESTAURANT/FOOD SERVICE

**Just a Shot Away**
297 N 1st St. #C
Kalama     360 673 6588
Open 6:00 a.m. to 2:00 p.m. M-F
8:00 a.m. to 2:00 p.m. Saturday

**Playa Azul II**                              B/L/D
262 NE Frontage Rd
Kalama     360 673 5067

**Hoopla's**                                   B/L/D
Fir and N 1st St.
Kalama     360 817 2408
www.hooplas.info

**Kalama Shopping Center**
223 N 1st St.
Kalama     360 673 2200

**Poker Pete's Pizza**                         L/D
164 N 1st
Kalama     360 673 3240

**Subway**                                     B/L/D
550 N 1st St.
Kalama     360 673 7474

### from EXIT 27

**Rebel Truck Stop**                           B/L/D
7349 Old Pacific Hwy S.
Kalama     360 673 2885

77

# SHOPPING – Exit 30 KALAMA

### Rivertown Antique Market
155 Elm Street
Kalama          360 673 2263
*Wide variety of antiques*

### Green Mountain Gifts
175 N. 1st
Kalama          360 673 4009
*Gifts, cards, candles, etc..*

### Heritage Square
176 N. 1st
Kalama          360 673 3980
*Gifts, antiques*

### Old Friends Antiques
297 N 1st
Kalama          360 673 3223
*Antiques and furniture*

### Good Day Market
334 1st Street
Kalama          360 673 4546
Food * Gasoline * Coffee * Gifts

### Columbia Antique Mall
364 N. 1st St.
Kalama          360 673 5400
*Antiques*

## Double D's Feed Store
384 N. 1st Street
Kalama
*Pet, large animal supplies*

## SERVICE ORGANIZATIONS

### AMALAK Women's Club
PO Box 883
Kalama, WA    98625          360 673 2281

### Kalama Lions Club
Called to order on January 25, 1940
Meets 4th Monday of August to 2nd Monday of June
7:00 p.m. dinner meeting at Community Building
PO Box 926
Kalama, WA    98625          360 673 5307

### IOOF No 101
Founded May 12, 1892
Meeting 2nd & 4th Wednesdays
Entrance at rear of IOOF building.
222 N 1st
Kalama, WA 98625             360 673 3581

### Kalama VFW
Meets 1st Thursday
IOOF Hall on 11st
Kalama, WA 98625             360 673 5146

## TOWING

**J & B Towing Services**
116 Wilson Drive
Kalama, WA    360 673 4030

# CALENDAR OF EVENTS

FEBRUARY
    2nd Weekend – **Antique Wheel and Deal** hosted by stores in downtown Kalama

MARCH – Chamber Dinner

APRIL
    *Lion's Club Easter Egg Hunt Saturday before EASTER at Camp Kalama*

MAY
    1st Weekend Kress Lake Fishing Derby Exit 32 - North of Fairgrounds

JUNE
    1st Saturday of month **Farmer's Market** begins
    First Weekend **Kalama Art Walk**
    Both events are held in downtown Kalama

JULY
    2nd Weekend **Kalama Community Fair** and Parade
    Exit 32 for Fairgrounds

AUGUST
    2nd Weekend Lion's Club **Garage Sale** at Lion's Club Building/Helping Hand off Cloverdale Road
    3rd Weekend All City **Yard Sale**
Kalama's **Days of Discovery** - multiple events are scheduled.
Complete calendar at www.cityofkalama.com
3rd Sunday **Classic Car Show** sponsored by the Chamber of Commerce and Untouchables Car Club on Main Street.
*Food, Entertainment, Music, Games*

SEPTEMBER
   2nd Weekend – **Antique Wheel and Deal**

OCTOBER
   1st Saturday – last **Farmer's Market** on Main Street
   31st Halloween – Trick or Treat Downtown

NOVEMBER
Kalama United Methodist Church Bazaar at 2nd and Elm St.

DECEMBER
   1st weekend – Christmas Parade, Santa Claus, Tree lighting ceremony at Toteff Park, Christmas Dinner by Amalak held at the Elementary School
   24th – Fire District #5 Santa Cruz - Santa cruises the surrounding neighborhoods and country roads in a fire truck!

Christmas in Kalama is a three-day event beginning the first Friday evening in December with Christmas caroling at Toteff Park. Saturday afternoon the children have their picture taken with Santa at the Community Building. On Sunday evening the community is invited to the school for a traditional Christmas dinner. Each child receives a special gift from Santa (and sometimes his wife!) donated by Kalama businesses.

To learn more about up coming events visit us at

www.cityofkalama.com

City of Kalama (360) 673-5562
Chamber of Commerce (360) 673-6299

## Kalama 2025

In 2025 Kalama, nestled between the Columbia and Kalama Rivers, will be a town that knows where it's going ... and proud of where it's been. Its historical downtown core boasts a thriving business center located within a picturesque setting frozen in time. Downtown merchants and patrons enjoy the hometown feeling created more than a century ago. Consistent attractive architecture, lighting and landscaping, parks and vistas make downtown a destination for residents and visitors.

Due to partnerships and collaboration this intergenerational community has developed expanded cultural venues, activity centers and educational opportunities for residents of all ages.

In Kalama all enjoy a tight-knit sense of community. Whether frequent I-5 commuters or overnight tourists attending one of the many year-round events and festivals, Kalama happily greets the traveler with a friendly smile and hometown charm. Kalama provides for many a home away from home.

In the year 2025 as in the years before Kalama is a town where all generations have a place, and a place people will proudly call home.

Be sure to visit

# KALAMA

## WHERE HIGHWAY, RAIL AND WATER MEET

Exits 27, 30 and 32
off Interstate 5
in the
Evergreen State of
**WASHINGTON**

# Index

## A

Alford, Richard and Carmen 66
AMALAK Women's Club 79, 82
Antique District 44, 67-68
Antique Wheel and Deal 81–82
Art Walk 81
ATM 68

## B

Bandy, David C. 65
Benny, Jack 17
Blackman, Frank 64

## C

Campbell, Susy 54
Cemetery 69
Chamber of Commerce 81, 82
Chief Lelooska 19–20
China Garden 17, 27
Church of the Nazarene 63
Classic Car Show 81
Cloverdale Road 17
Coffey, George 23, 28
Columbia River 16
Community Building 41–43, 63, 74, 82
Community Fair 81
Cowlitz County Museum 54
Cowlitz River 24–28

## D

Darnell Mine 28
Day, Robert 22, 27
Days of Discovey 25–28
Dunn family 49

Duvall, George  46

# E

Eader, Wes  66
Elm Street  37

# F

Farmer's Market  81–82
Fire  62–66
Fish  72
fish hatchery  16–18
Fishing  60

# G

Gore, George  47
Green Mountain Road  17
Grubbs, Walter  65

# I

Imus family  35
Imus, Hite  27
IOOF No 101  79

# K

Kalama Baptist Church  65
Kalama Fairgrounds  25
Kalama High School  17, 36
Kalama, John  22, 24
Kalama Marine Park  20
Kalama River  17–18
Kalama School District  71
Kalama Telephone  28
Kalama United Methodist Church  62
Kazano House  41
Kockritz  44, 56

# L

Larson, John  48
Library  71

Lions Club 79, 81
Lodging 71
Lozier, Jerry and Sherry 66

# M

Marina 18, 73
Martin's Bluff 24
Masonic Lodge 38
Meeker Drive 17–18
Meeker, Ezra 15, 22, 25
Military Road 17–18
Minnetonka 22–23, 26–28
Modrow 17–18

# N

Newman, Mike 66
Northern Pacific Railroad 15–18, 24
Northern Pacific Railroad Hospital 32–43

# O

Orem, Chester 64

# P

Park 72
Presley, Elvis 17

# R

Recreation 71
Restaurant 75
Roosevelt, Theodore 17, 60
RV Park 72

# S

Salisbury, Pastor 65
Second Avenue 31
Seibert, John 39
Shopping 78
St. Joseph's Catholic Church 17–18, 37, 61

Storie Mansion 35
Suddeth, Mel 66

## T

Tacoma 26–28, 57, 62
Taft, Howard 17
totem pole 19

## V

VFW 79

## W

W., H. Kockritz 44
Westerlund, Myrtle 64